MINI PETS

Tadpoles

By Theresa Greenaway

Photographs by Chris Fairclough

RSVP

RAINTREE
STECK-VAUGHN
PUBLISHERS
A Steck-Vaughn Company

Austin, Texas

www.steck-vaughn.com

Published by Raintree Steck-Vaughn Publishers, an imprint of Steck-Vaughn Company.

Project Editors: Patience Coster, Pam Wells
Project Manager: Joyce Spicer
Illustrated by Colin Newman and Stefan Chabluk
Designed by Ian Winton

Planned and produced by Discovery Books Limited.

Library of Congress Cataloging-in-Publication Data
Greenaway, Theresa, 1947-
Tadpoles / by Theresa Greenaway; photography by Chris Fairclough.
p.   cm. — (Minipets)
Includes bibliographical references (p. 30) and index.
Summary: Provides information on the identification, life cycle, and habitats of tadpoles, as well as on how to collect and care for them as pets.
ISBN 0-7398-1828-7 (hardcover)
ISBN 0-7398-2195-4 (softcover)
1. Tadpoles as pets Juvenile literature. [1. Tadpoles. 2. Tadpoles as pets.
3. Frogs.   4. Toads.   5. Pets.] I. Fairclough, Chris, ill.   II. Title.   III. Series:
Greenaway, Theresa, 1947-   Minipets.
SF459.T35G74   2000
639.3'789—dc21   99-37301
CIP

1 2 3 4 5 6 7 8 9 0 LB 03 02 01 00 99
Printed and bound in the United States of America.

Words explained in the glossary appear in **bold** the first time they are used in the text.

Contents

Introducing Tadpoles   4

Finding Tadpoles   6

Tadpole Collecting   8

Homes for Tadpoles   10

Watching Them Grow   12

Caring for Tadpoles   14

Feeding Tadpoles   16

Tadpole Behavior   18

Staying Alive   20

Leaving the Water   22

Keeping a Record   24

Letting Them Go   26

Frog and Tadpole Facts   28

Further Reading   30

Glossary   31

Index   32

Introducing Tadpoles

Tadpoles make wonderful minipets. Most kinds of tadpoles live in water. They are the **larvae**, or young, of frogs and toads.

A young tadpole does not look anything like its frog or toad parents. It has a round or oval body, and a long tail. There is a wide fin along the top and bottom of the tail. For the first stages of its life, a tadpole has no arms or legs. It can only move by wiggling its tail.

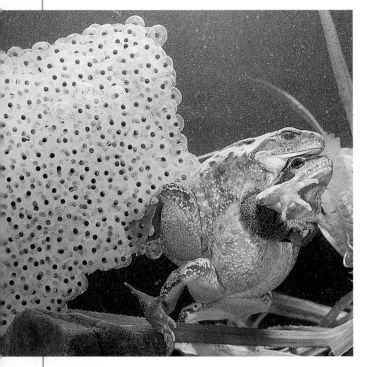

Tadpoles hatch from eggs. Each egg is made up of a tiny **embryo** surrounded by jelly. The jelly helps to protect the embryo from hungry enemies. Frogs often lay their eggs in one big mass, called spawn. Toad spawn is often laid in strings.

◄ As the female frog lays her eggs, they are fertilized by the male. Only eggs that have been fertilized will develop into tadpoles.

Gradually, tadpoles change into frogs or toads that are tiny copies of their parents. This usually takes two to four months. By keeping tadpoles as minipets, you will be able to watch each stage of this amazing change.

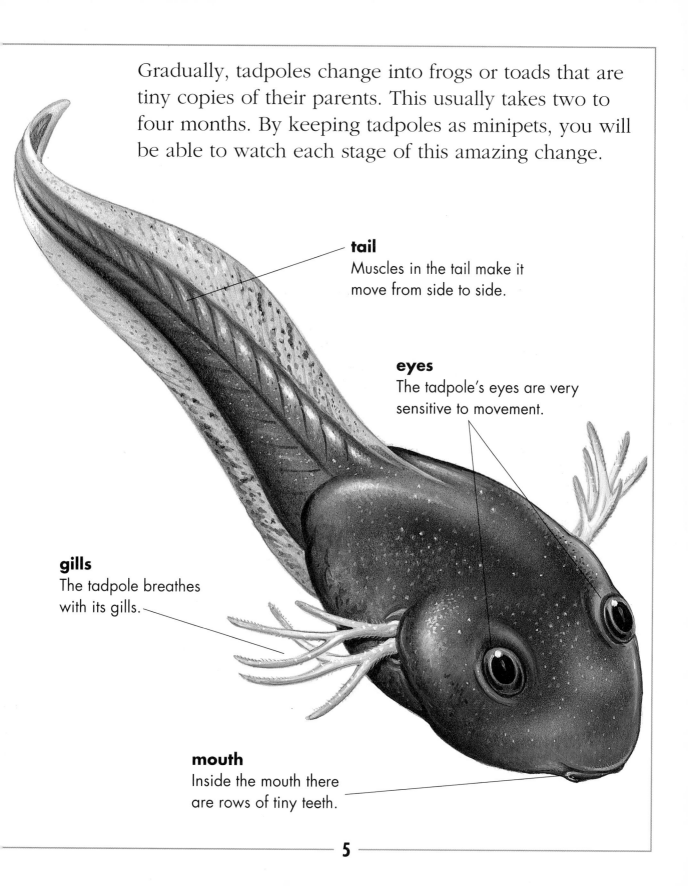

tail
Muscles in the tail make it move from side to side.

eyes
The tadpole's eyes are very sensitive to movement.

gills
The tadpole breathes with its gills.

mouth
Inside the mouth there are rows of tiny teeth.

Finding Tadpoles

Most tadpoles live in water. Their delicate skin must be kept moist, or they will dry out and die. Frogs and toads are found in most parts of the world. They are not found in the ocean or where it is too cold or dry. They may be found a long way from the nearest pond. But they all have to return to water to breed.

◀ Inside each egg in this picture, there is a tiny tadpole that is almost ready to hatch.

Spring is the best time of year to start looking for spawn or tadpoles. Many frogs and toads lay their eggs in spring, all at once. Others lay smaller amounts throughout the summer. These eggs are much harder to find. They may be hidden underneath leaves and rocks, or just scattered over the bottom of the pond.

If you have a garden pond, look there first. If you do not have a pond, then start hunting in ponds, streams, and ditches near where you live. Do not go exploring ponds on your own. Make sure a grown-up comes with you. If no tadpoles can be seen at first, keep still and wait. They may be hiding.

Tadpoles in trees

Tropical gray tree frogs from Africa spawn in branches that hang over ponds. Their eggs are covered in a slimy liquid. The frogs beat this liquid into a mass of bubbles or stiff froth. The froth dries and hardens around the mass of eggs. When the tadpoles hatch, they wriggle free and fall into water below.

Tadpole Collecting

If you collect some frog or toad spawn, you can watch your tadpoles hatch. First, you will need a small net with a long handle. Then, you will need some jars or other waterproof containers with holes in the lids. You will also need a notebook and pencil to write down where you found your new pets and the date you found them.

With a container, scoop out some spawn or tadpoles near the edge of the water. If the spawn is farther out, then a grown-up can use the net to collect it. Once the spawn or tadpoles are in the container, put the lid on. Now collect some of the pondweed growing in the water. You will need this for your pets' new home. Put it into another container.

What a mouthful!

The Darwin's frog lays its eggs on land. The male frog guards the eggs until the tadpoles start to wiggle inside. He then "swallows" them and keeps the eggs safe inside in his vocal sacs (throat pouches). Three weeks later, when the eggs have developed into tiny frogs, the male frog spits them out to fend for themselves.

Do not take all the spawn or tadpoles from the pond or stream. They are part of the natural wildlife there.

Identifying tadpoles is very difficult, even for experts. Do not worry if you cannot identify yours. Part of the fun of keeping tadpoles is waiting to see what they turn into when they grow up.

Homes for Tadpoles

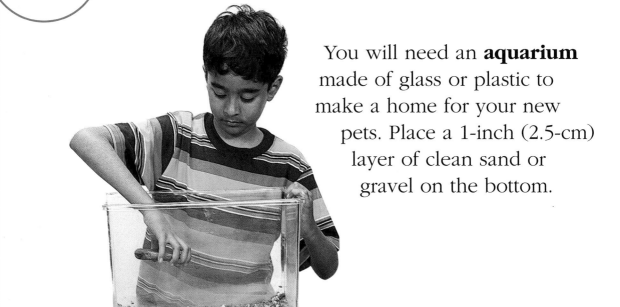

You will need an **aquarium** made of glass or plastic to make a home for your new pets. Place a 1-inch (2.5-cm) layer of clean sand or gravel on the bottom.

pondweed

clay flowerpot

large pebbles

lid

clean sand or gravel

Now you need to make places for the tadpoles
to find shelter or look for food. Add a few large
pebbles and a clay flowerpot on its side.
Then fill the aquarium with pond
or rainwater.

Put plenty of pondweed into the
aquarium. The pondweed can be
tied to a stone, so that it roots in
the sand or gravel. Or it can
float near the surface.

▶ Empty the
container of spawn
into its new home.

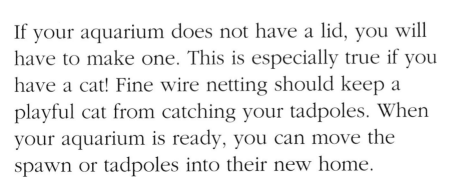

If your aquarium does not have a lid, you will
have to make one. This is especially true if you
have a cat! Fine wire netting should keep a
playful cat from catching your tadpoles. When
your aquarium is ready, you can move the
spawn or tadpoles into their new home.

Watching Them Grow

If you have collected spawn, look at it carefully every day. Inside its thick layer of jelly, the tiny embryo in each egg soon starts to grow. After about fourteen days, the tiny tadpoles wriggle out of their jelly. Newly-hatched tadpoles are very small and look just like black commas.

You will see tiny, feathery **gills** on each side of the tadpole. These gills **absorb** the oxygen in the water. They allow the tadpole to breathe underwater. As the tadpole grows, its gills become covered by a flap of skin.

The growing tadpole

1. The young tadpole has gills.

2. The gills are gradually covered by a flap of skin.

3. The hind legs appear first.

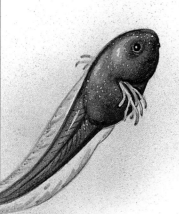

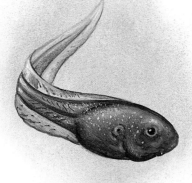

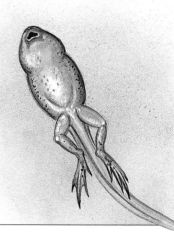

If you look at the tadpole's gills with a magnifying glass, you may be able to see the flaps opening and closing as it breathes.

▼ Only very young tadpoles have feathery gills on each side of their bodies.

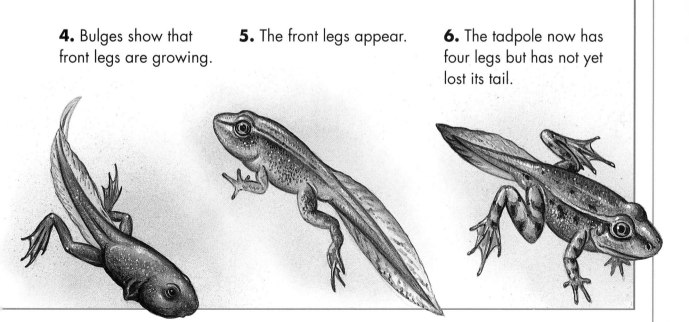

4. Bulges show that front legs are growing.

5. The front legs appear.

6. The tadpole now has four legs but has not yet lost its tail.

Caring for Tadpoles

Tadpoles are easy to look after, but there are some things to remember. Your pets will be happiest if their new home is as much like their old home as possible. If the pond that the tadpoles came from was cold, then their aquarium needs to be kept cool. Make sure it is not in direct sunlight.

Backpacking frog

The marsupial frog is from the tropical rain forests of Central and South America. The male pushes the female's eggs into a pouch on her back. Here they hatch into tadpoles. After three to four months, she releases the tadpoles into a pond or ditch.

As your tadpoles grow, you will need to start feeding them tiny pieces of raw meat. But their water must be kept clean. Take out any uneaten food every day, otherwise it will go bad. Change the water if it starts to smell. To do this, take a jug or old mug and carefully scoop out the old water and pour it away. Make sure you do not accidentally catch your tadpoles in the jug as well! When you have scooped out most of the old water, to a depth of about 1 inch (2.5 cm), slowly pour in the fresh water.

Remember to replace the lid. If you keep your aquarium outside, protect it from rain. Otherwise it will overflow, and the tadpoles could be washed away.

Feeding Tadpoles

Tiny tadpoles do not swim around much. They feed on the film of tiny living things that grow on the surface of underwater stones and leaves. You would need a microscope to see what they eat. As they grow, the tadpoles become more active, but they still get much of their food by nibbling off this slimy layer.

Larger tadpoles are **scavengers**. They eat dead pond animals and creatures like slugs and worms that have fallen in and drowned. Sometimes tadpoles attack and eat each other.

▲ A dead fish provides plenty of food for this group of tadpoles.

In an aquarium, the tadpoles will search in the pondweed for food. They will also soon start to nibble from the pieces of raw meat you have given them. Watch a tadpole while it feeds. Use a magnifying glass to look for the tiny rows of teeth around its mouth. Do not give your tadpoles too much meat because it will rot and make the water smell awful. Tadpoles will die if their water is stale.

Caring parent

Some kinds of poison arrow frogs feed their tadpoles. The female puts one or two tadpoles in little "water tanks" in the cupped leaves of plants that grow high up on the branches of tropical rain forest trees. Every few days she returns to lay an egg that will not grow in the "tank." The little tadpoles feed on this egg.

Tadpole Behavior

Without a tail, a tadpole could not move at all. Tadpoles can only swim by wiggling their long tails from side to side. This drives the heavy head and body through the water quite quickly. But they cannot swim as fast as a fish can. A tadpole also uses its tail to change direction. Can you see how it does this?

Watch tadpoles swimming around quietly. Then, see how fast they move if they are alarmed. What frightens tadpoles? Try making a sudden movement, like clapping your hands, over the aquarium. Your tadpoles will dive to the bottom or hide in the weeds. They do this because they think a bird is about to peck them out of the water with its bill. Do your tadpoles generally stay together in a group? Or do they scatter throughout the water?

Survival of the fittest

North American spadefoot toads have two types of tadpoles. The first type eats bits of plant material. The second type develops strong jaws that help it catch and eat other water animals. It may even eat the plant-eating spadefoot tadpoles. Spadefoot tadpoles live in small desert pools that dry up after about three weeks, so they have to grow really quickly. Only the strongest tadpoles survive.

Some pet shops sell tadpoles from other parts of the world. You might want to try keeping some of these. If you have more than one kind of tadpole, you can compare their behavior.

Staying Alive

Tadpoles have plump bodies with soft skin. To all kinds of other hungry animals, a tadpole is a really tasty meal. Fish, birds, newts, and some turtles all eat tadpoles. You may be surprised to learn that one tadpole **predator** is an insect—a diving beetle. The larvae and adult beetle are both fierce hunters. They live in ponds and will catch and eat many tadpoles.

▲ A diving beetle larva bites into a tadpole with its large, powerful jaws.

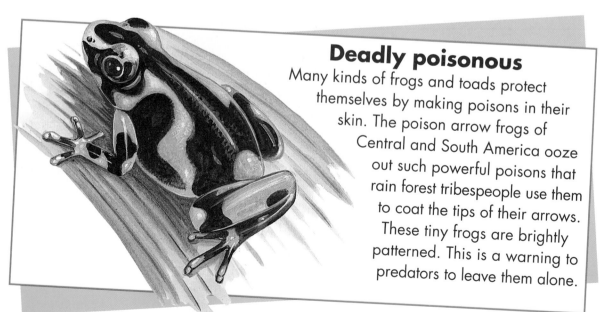

Deadly poisonous

Many kinds of frogs and toads protect themselves by making poisons in their skin. The poison arrow frogs of Central and South America ooze out such powerful poisons that rain forest tribespeople use them to coat the tips of their arrows. These tiny frogs are brightly patterned. This is a warning to predators to leave them alone.

With so many predators, it is amazing that any tadpoles survive! But the female frog or toad lays lots of eggs. This allows for some to be eaten. Tiny tadpoles hide among patches of thick pondweed. Many kinds of tadpoles stay together in a group, so that their wriggling tails confuse a predator.

▼ A tadpole that is speckled with brown spots may look just like a dead stem if it keeps still.

As they grow larger, tadpoles often change color so that they blend in with their background. This is called **camouflage**. If tadpoles keep very still, it is hard for an enemy to find them.

Leaving the Water

As it grows, the tadpole's mouth and the shape of its head become more froglike. The eyes begin to bulge. Then, the tail gradually shrinks. The tadpole starts to use its hind legs to swim. By the time the front legs have appeared, little lungs have developed inside the tadpole's body to replace the gills. Your tadpole has turned into a tiny frog or toad. The young frog or toad needs to swim up to the surface of the water to gulp in air.

▲ This tiny frog is climbing out of the water for the first time.

Sticky feet

Tree frogs live in the green leaves of bushes and trees. Some kinds only come down to the ground to breed. As soon as tiny green tree frogs leave the water, they start to climb. They have sticky pads on their long toes. These help them to grip as they climb higher and higher.

In the wild, tiny frogs and toads climb out of the pool and sit on the side among the shady plants. Yours may try to climb up the sides of the aquarium. Float a piece of bark or wood on the surface of the water. The small frogs or toads will climb onto this. They want to leave the water, but they still need somewhere damp to live.

You will need a different home for your pets now. It should have much less water and plenty of damp moss. Add some plants or stones where the frogs can hide. Young frogs and toads need even tinier living insects and small earthworms to eat.

Keeping a Record

Your tadpoles will change a little bit every day. Some may grow faster than others. Keep a record in your nature notebook. Write down the dates that you notice all the changes in your pets.

Keeping tadpoles and watching them grow is fun, but there is a lot that you can learn, too. Even scientists do not know very much about tadpole behavior. Your notes will help you remember how your tadpole pets changed into frogs or toads.

Tadpoles

Spawn found: in garden pond
Date: April 2

My tiny tadpoles are still in their jelly.

I kept my tadpoles in an aquarium, like this.

My tadpoles have grown hind legs.
Date: June 3

You might want to find out more about tadpoles, and the toads and frogs that they become. There are plenty of books about these **amphibians**, so have a good look in your library. Other sources of information are CD-ROM encyclopedias and the Internet. You could join a wildlife club, or start a club with some friends.

Amphibians galore!

There are over 3,500 different kinds of frogs and toads alive in the world today. Some of these have become quite rare because people have destroyed their natural **habitats**. The tomato frog from Madagascar was in danger of becoming extinct, or dying out. But it is now being bred in zoos.

Letting Them Go

You can keep your pets even after they have turned into frogs or toads. But frogs and toads need a different kind of home from tadpoles, and they only eat living, moving prey. Such prey can be hard to find, especially in winter. This is why frogs and toads **hibernate** in places that have cold winters.

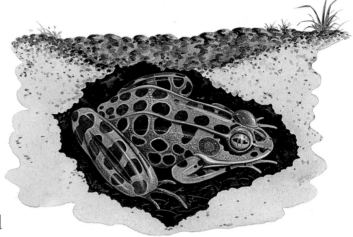

▲ Frogs and toads may burrow into damp soil or wet mud to spend the winter.

You may decide you no longer want to keep your tadpoles, or the frogs or toads they have become. Then, you must take them back to the place where you found them. Check your notebook to be sure where to return them. Gently empty their container into the pond or stream and watch them swim away.

◀ As the frogs or toads are released into the pond, they will quickly hide among pondweeds.

A fragile balance

Setting foreign species of frogs and toads free in the wild can cause problems. South American cane toads were taken to Australia in 1935 to control insects that were eating sugarcane. These big, poisonous toads breed very quickly. They have no natural predators in Australia. Soon there were so many of them, eating so much, that they upset the balance of nature.

If you have bought foreign frog or toad tadpoles from a pet shop, these must not be set free in the wild.

▶ When a frog sees a moving insect, it takes aim and catches it with a long, sticky tongue.

Frog and Tadpole Facts

Tadpoles of the Australian hidden-ear frog and long-footed frog can survive in pools where the water reaches 104 degrees Farenheit (40° C).

▲ The hidden-ear frog's eardrum is covered by a flap of skin.

The largest frog in the world is the goliath frog. It lives in Africa and can eat small birds and mice.

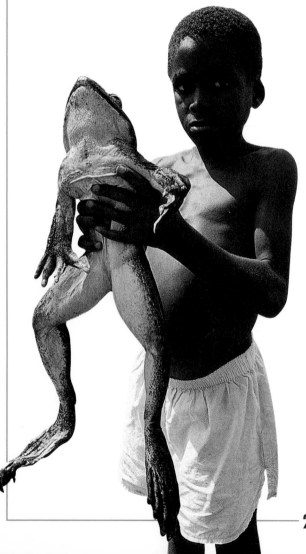

◀ A full-grown goliath frog has a body that is at least 12 inches (30 cm) long. If it stretches out its back legs, it looks even longer!

The tadpoles of the shrinking frog grow to a giant 8 inches (20 cm), but when they turn into frogs, they "shrink" to 3 inches (8 cm).

Some tropical Central and South America frogs lay their eggs in damp leaf litter on the forest floor. Inside each egg, a tiny frog develops. When it hatches, it is fully formed.

The tailed frog lives in cold mountain streams on the western slopes of the Cascade Mountains in the United States. Its tadpoles take as long as three years to change into frogs.

▼ This torrent frog tadpole can feed without being washed away by fast-flowing water.

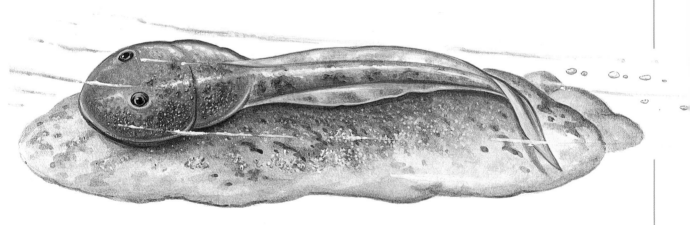

The tadpoles of the torrent frog of Southeast Asia have large suckers underneath their bodies. They use these to cling to rocks. This way, they avoid being washed away by the fast-moving water of tropical streams.

Further Reading

Crewe, Sabrina. *The Frog* (Life Cycles series). Raintree Steck-Vaughn, 1997.

Dewey, Jennifer O. *Poison Dart Frogs.* Boyds Mills Press, 1998.

Johnson, Sylvia. *Tree Frogs.* Lerner, 1986.

Kellogg, Steven. *Mysterious Tadpole: Book and Toy in a Jar.* Dial, 1997.

Lovett, Sarah. *Extremely Weird Frogs.* John Muir, 1996.

Patent, Dorothy H. *Flashy Fantastic Rain Forest Frogs.* Walker, 1997.

Pfeffer, Wendy. *From Tadpole to Frog* (Let's-Read-and-Find-Out Science Books series). HarperCollins Children's Books, 1994.

Stewart, David E., and Scrayce, Carolyn. *From Tadpole to Frog* (Lifecycles series). Children's Press, 1998.

Glossary

Absorb To take in.

Amphibian A cold-blooded animal that lives on land but breeds in water.

Aquarium A container, or tank, where small animals can be kept.

Camouflage The coloring of an animal that helps it to blend in with its surroundings.

Embryo An animal in the early stages of development.

Gill Part of a young tadpole's body, through which it breathes.

Habitat The natural home of an animal.

Hibernate To sleep through the cold months of the year.

Larvae Tadpoles, or the young of frogs and toads.

Predator An animal that eats other living creatures.

Scavenger An animal that feeds on scraps of dead plants or dead animals.

Index

amphibians 25
Australian hidden-ear frog 28
Australian long-footed frog 28

behavior 18-19

camouflage 21

Darwin's frog 9
defense 21

embryo 4, 12

feeding 15, 16-17, 19, 23, 27

gills 12-13
goliath frog 28

hibernation 26
homes for tadpoles 10-11

marsupial frog 14
mating 4

North American spadefoot toad
    19

poison arrow frog 17, 20
predators 20-21, 27
prey 26

shrinking frog 29
South American cane toad 27
spawn 4, 6-9, 11, 12

tailed frog 29
tomato frog 25
torrent frog tadpole 29
tree frog 22
tropical gray tree frog 7

The publishers would like to thank the following for their permission to reproduce photographs:
Cover (tadpoles) Kim Taylor/Bruce Coleman, 4 Jane Burton/Bruce Coleman, 6 W Meinderts/Foto Natura/Frank Lane Picture Agency, 7 bottom K G Preston-Mafham/Premaphotos Wildlife, 9 Michael Fogden/Oxford Scientific Films, 13 W Meinderts/Foto Natura/Frank Lane Picture Agency, 14 M P L Fogden/Bruce Coleman, 16 Jane Burton/Bruce Coleman, 17 bottom M P L Fogden/Bruce Coleman, 19 Roger Jackman/Oxford Scientific Films, 20 top G I Bernard/Oxford Scientific Films, 21 Jane Burton/Bruce Coleman, 22 top Jane Burton/Bruce Coleman, 25 Zig Leszczynski/Oxford Scientific Films, 27 Joe Macdonald/Bruce Coleman, 28 Daniel Heuclin/NHPA.
With thanks to Bob and Susie Cunning for the use of their pond.